Contents

China: Unpacked

Welcome to China, the country that's hard to ignore! It's BIG on a map, BUZZING with people and BOOMING with business and trade. Get ready for a world of tea and chopsticks, skyscrapers and shopping malls, dancing dragons and kung fu fighters. Walk the Great Wall, ride a lightning-fast train or challenge a ping-pong pro to a game. This fascinating place attracts over 55 million visitors a year — so let's unpack and join the crowds!

Fact file

Flag: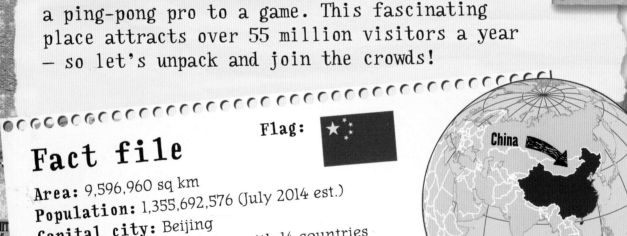

Area: 9,596,960 sq km
Population: 1,355,692,576 (July 2014 est.)
Capital city: Beijing
Land borders: 22,457km with 14 countries
Currency: Renminbi/Yuan
Official language: Standard Mandarin

China

3 0132 02477717 4

NORTHUMBERLAND COUNTY LIBRARY

You should return this book on or before the last date stamped
below unless an extension of the loan period is granted.

Application for renewal may be made by letter or telephone.

Fines at the approved rate will be charged when a book is
overdue.

ASHINGTON

10-17

HALTWHISTLE

10|23

WAYLAND
www.waylandbooks.co.uk

Published in paperback in 2017 by Wayland
Copyright © Hodder and Stoughton, 2017

All rights reserved

Editor: Nicola Edwards
Designer: Peter Clayman
Cover design: Matthew Kelly

Dewey number: 951'.0612-dc23
ISBN: 978 0 7502 9174 3

Wayland, an imprint of
Hachette Children's Group
Part of Hodder and Stoughton
Carmelite House
50 Victoria Embankment
London EC4Y 0DZ

An Hachette UK Company
www.hachette.co.uk
www.hachettechildrens.co.uk

Printed and bound in Singapore

10 9 8 7 6 5 4 3 2 1

Picture acknowledgements: All images and graphic elements courtesy of Shutterstock except
p 7 (t), p9 (b), p17 (r), p19 (t), p22 Corbis.com and p25 (t) Wikimedia Commons

Every attempt has been made to clear copyright. Should there be any inadvertent omission,
please apply to the publisher for rectification.

The website addresses (URLs) included in this book were valid at the time of
going to press. However, it is possible that contents or addresses may have
changed since the publication of this book. No responsibility for any such
changes can be accepted by either the author or the Publisher.

You can see on this map the land borders that China shares with other countries. China's capital, Beijing, is shown too, along with some of the other places you can read about in this book.

Russia

Mongolia

Kyrgyzstan

Tajikistan

Pakistan

China

Nepal

Bhutan

Bangladesh

India

Myanmar

Thailand

Laos

Vietnam

Yellow

Beijing

Xi'an

Three Gorges Dam

Yangtze

Pearl

Guangzhou

Hong Kong

South China Sea

North Korea

South Korea

Japan

Yellow Sea

Shanghai

East China Sea

Taiwan

牛
ox

龍
dragon

馬
horse

羊
ram

兔
rabbit

蛇
snake

豬
boar

鼠
mouse

狗
dog

虎
tiger

猴
monkey

雞
rooster

To write Chinese, you have to learn THOUSANDS of characters like these!

China is home to half of the world's pigs – about 500 million of them!

The Story of China

It may be the fastest developing country in history, but there's nothing new about China! It was home to one of the oldest civilizations on the planet, dating back more than 4,000 years. China has hundreds of wars, endless inventions and centuries of culture under its belt. Now a record-breaking 1.3 billion people live in China — and they're taking the world by storm.

NO WAY!

The ancient Chinese invented ice cream (from a mixture of milk, rice and snow) as well as gunpowder. Talk about sweet and sour!

Emperor Puyi (right) literally toddled to the throne.

The People's Republic

In 1949, after years of civil war, Mao Zedong and his Communist Party founded the People's Republic of China. Mao set up state-owned industry and collective farms, reshaping society to be more equal. He outlawed religion and sent teachers to labour camps. Tens of millions of people starved to death under his rule. Even so, Mao is seen as a hero for modernizing China, which is still a communist state today.

Family Power

Before 1911, China was ruled by a series of families, or dynasties, led by a string of emperors. The longest-lasting was the Han Dynasty (206 BCE–220 CE) – a great time for the arts and trade. In 690, China's only female emperor, Wu Zetian, came to power after toppling various rivals. The last emperor, Puyi, took the throne in 1908 when he was just two years old! At the age of six, he was overthrown and China was declared a republic.

Mao died in 1976, but you can still see his portrait in Beijing's Tiananmen Square.

The Great Wall

The Great Wall of China tells a story that spans more than 2,000 years. It began when China's first emperor (in around 220 BCE) ordered existing walls to be joined, as a barrier against northern invaders. In the 1300s, the Ming Dynasty rebuilt and lengthened the wall. It's still the biggest human-made structure on Earth, winding in broken sections for over 20,000km.

How is the Great Wall held together? By mortar mixed with sticky rice!

One in a Billion

A fifth of all people on the planet live in China – so what's it like to be one of them? Firstly, get used to the crowds! With over 40,000 babies born every day, this is one chockablock country (at least in the built-up parts). There's competition for space, jobs, food and overall success, but respect for others is important here, and family life and friendships are prized.

School Slog

Education is a mark of success in China, and students are under pressure to do well. Chinese pupils have longer days and shorter holidays than most children in the West – many go to cramming lessons in the evenings and at weekends. In some regions, children as young as three are sent away to boarding school. For rural pupils, the nearest school may be so far away that boarding is the only option.

Chinese schools get some of the best results in the world.

Sibling-Free!

In 1979, the Chinese government decided that the country couldn't cope with its growing population. They made it the law that each family could have only one child. Nowadays couples may have a second baby if one parent is an only-child, or in rural areas if the first-born is a girl. The policy has left China with an ageing population — by 2050, one in four people will be 60 or over.

The children of one-child families are known as 'Little Emperors' in China.

NO WAY!

Chinese children are often named after events. Thousands are called Aoyun, meaning 'Olympic Games', which took place in 2008 in Beijing!

Out and About

Chinese families like to get out and about in their spare time. During weekends and holidays, attractions such as the Great Wall can be jam-packed. Many people head to parks or squares to fly kites or play traditional games like mahjong. As wealth increases, travel is becoming popular, too. By 2020, Chinese tourists are expected to make 100 million overseas trips a year — more than any other nation.

Sichuan province's 'Dead Sea' pool can cram in 15,000 people!

Futuristic Cities

China is the place to come for huge, happening and hectic cities. At least 160 of them have over a million people, and five are home to 10 million or more. New metropolises are springing up - some, like Ordos in Inner Mongolia, are still almost empty. But China's thriving cities gleam with opportunity, despite a veil of smog from factories and heaving traffic.

Between 1420 and 1911, 24 emperors lived in the Forbidden City.

Booming Beijing

Beijing is China's capital city, and it's been the seat of power for most of the last 1,000 years. You can step right back to the days of the dynasties in the Forbidden City, the Temple of Heaven and the Summer Palace. Tiananmen Square is one of the world's biggest city squares – it can hold a million people. Head there at sunrise to see the national flag-raising ceremony (if you're awake!).

The Shanghai Tower is the tall, tube-like building on the right.

Showcase Shanghai

Over 24 million people live in the biggest Chinese city, Shanghai. This showcase for China's boom times also boasts the world's biggest container port. You can whizz around on one of the busiest ever metros, the oldest trolleybus system or a super-fast train (see p16). Stroll down The Bund, a historic waterfront – or crane your neck at one of the world's tallest buildings, the Shanghai Tower.

Hectic Hong Kong

The island-studded city of Hong Kong, once governed by Britain, has a degree of separate rule from China. It's a shiny, swarming world finance centre, where people live in tiny flats packed into towering blocks. If you're lucky enough to visit, check out the famous skyline from a tram chugging up Victoria Peak – and be sure to have a great time at a fun park, designer mall or beach.

You get an amazing view of Hong Kong from the Victoria Peak tram.

NO WAY!

Over the past few years, China has built a new skyscraper every five days!

A World in One

You can fit a whole world of landscapes and climates into a country as big as China! Get ready for subarctic cold, tropical heat, desert droughts and monsoon rains. There are mighty mountains, great rivers and more than 5,000 islands here. China is sometimes described as a staircase with three steps, climbing from low plains in the east to hills in the centre to high, icy peaks in the west.

Rushing Rivers

The Yangtze is the third-longest river in world, supplying water to many Chinese cities. Thanks to the Three Gorges Dam, it also produces electricity – though building the dam drowned thousands of towns, villages and ancient sites. The Yellow River gets its name from the colour of all the mud it picks up. It's also known as the River of Sorrow, as a result of many devastating floods.

Hydropower dams don't come bigger than the Three Gorges.

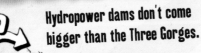

Mountains loom over the buildings of Kowloon, an area of Hong Kong.

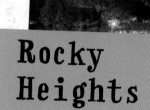

Sandy Storms

Imagine waking up to find your city caked in orange dust. China has more desert than farmland, and every spring winds whip up choking clouds of sand and carry them across the country. Thousands of tonnes of sand can be dumped on Beijing in one go – enough to close schools and cancel flights. Sometimes the sand blows as far as California, USA, more than 9,000 km away!

Rocky Heights

Good news if you like heights – mountains cover two-thirds of China! The Himalayas run along its southern border, including the world's highest peak, Mount Everest, where the region of Tibet meets Nepal. China also has several sacred mountains, regularly climbed by pilgrims. Legend says you'll live to be 100 if you climb Mount Tai's 7,000+ steps; or you could take the bus and cable car.

Sandstorms can turn Beijing orange!

NO WAY!

China used to cross five time zones, but in 1949 Chairman Mao decided to make the whole country the same. This means the sun can rise as late as 10am in parts of China.

Country Life

With more than a billion mouths to feed, farming is important in China. Nearly half the population lives in the countryside, growing crops and raising animals for meat. Many rural people produce just enough to eat, while others work on huge commercial farms. But life is tough in rural areas, and China's prosperous cities are tempting people away.

Keep picking! China produces nearly 2 million tonnes of tea a year.

Top Crops

You don't need to look far for all the tea in China – it's the world's biggest producer of leaves for this popular brew! Rice is even more widespread, taking up about a quarter of China's cultivated land. Sometimes ducks or fish are kept in the rice paddy fields to eat up weeds and pests. In cooler, drier parts of the country, wheat and maize are common crops.

Vanishing Villages

People are leaving China's villages – jobs in cities pay on average three times more. Tens of millions have already moved, and the rush to the cities continues. In 2012, the population balance tipped from rural to urban areas for the first time. Thousands of traditional villages have been abandoned or swallowed up by industrial sprawl. In many places, it's the elderly that are left behind.

The cave village of Lijiashan is a lot emptier than it used to be.

NO WAY!

About 30 million people in China live in house caves, called yaodong, dug into the hillsides.

Basic Homes

Typical rural families live in simple houses and cook over open fires. Running water isn't found everywhere, but most villages now have electricity. Many villagers grow their own rice or maize and vegetables, or keep livestock such as goats, chickens and pigs. In the mountains, villages can be very remote, meaning a long or treacherous walk to the nearest shop or school.

A farm worker and his son in a rural area of Guizhou, a mountainous region in the southwest of China.

Going Places

China's city streets roar and splutter with traffic as more and more people own cars. Train passengers now make more than 2 billion trips per year – Chinese railway lines could loop more than twice around the Earth! Planes fly between cities and buses brave rough rural roads. During peak holiday times, when everyone travels at once, public transport can be quite a squeeze.

FASTEST Trains

It used to take nearly 24 hours to get from Beijing to Guangzhou by train. Now, thanks to the world's biggest high-speed rail network, you can do it in a third of that time. Bullet trains race along at over 200km per hour. That's fast – until you get on the Shanghai Maglev, which runs from the giant city to its airport. It reaches speeds of up to 430km per hour!

The Shanghai Maglev was the world's fastest train until Japan beat the record in 2015.

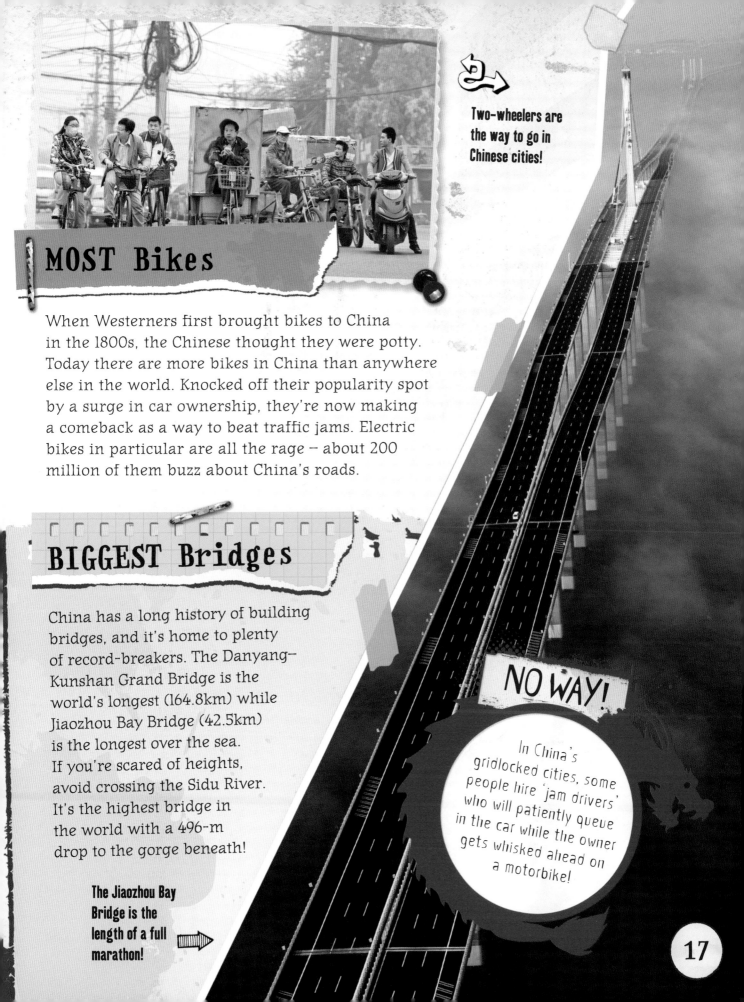

Two-wheelers are the way to go in Chinese cities!

MOST Bikes

When Westerners first brought bikes to China in the 1800s, the Chinese thought they were potty. Today there are more bikes in China than anywhere else in the world. Knocked off their popularity spot by a surge in car ownership, they're now making a comeback as a way to beat traffic jams. Electric bikes in particular are all the rage – about 200 million of them buzz about China's roads.

BIGGEST Bridges

China has a long history of building bridges, and it's home to plenty of record-breakers. The Danyang–Kunshan Grand Bridge is the world's longest (164.8km) while Jiaozhou Bay Bridge (42.5km) is the longest over the sea. If you're scared of heights, avoid crossing the Sidu River. It's the highest bridge in the world with a 496-m drop to the gorge beneath!

The Jiaozhou Bay Bridge is the length of a full marathon!

NO WAY!

In China's gridlocked cities, some people hire 'jam drivers' who will patiently queue in the car while the owner gets whisked ahead on a motorbike!

Ancient Arts

They invented paper — and ways to print on it — and they made the first porcelain and decorative silk. The ancient Chinese gave a lot to the creative world, and today's people have inherited their talents. From papercraft and painting to acrobatics and dance, China is a hotbed of colourful culture. Even Chinese writing, called calligraphy, is an art form in itself!

On Paper

Using just a brush and ink, Chinese artists can conjure up beautiful paintings. Nature is a favourite subject in Chinese art, from birds and flowers to mountains and trees. Jianzhi is the art of cutting paper into detailed symmetrical designs, often stuck onto windows. The Chinese also fold paper into fancy shapes (zhezhi), and craft it into colourful lanterns, fans or dragon puppets.

Paper dragons are an important part of Chinese New Year celebrations.

Born to Perform

If you can ride a unicycle, juggle just about anything or bend your toes over your ears, you could be ready for Chinese variety art. This age-old tradition involves a range of acrobatic and balancing acts. If music's more your thing, try Chinese opera. You get to wear crazy costumes and make-up and sing along to a gong or lute in a distinctive, high-pitched style.

Chinese opera is often sung in local dialects, with subtitles.

Say it in Clay

You might have guessed that china comes from China! Pottery has a long history here, from elaborate Ming vases to blue and white plates. When the first emperor, Qin Shi Huang, died, he wanted protection in the afterlife. So he ordered a whole army of 8,000 soldiers to be made out of clay for his tomb. Each soldier was different, and they carried real weapons too.

Qin's Terracotta Army was found by chance in 1974, by farmers in Xi'an digging a well!

Made in China

One reason modern China is booming is because we buy so much of their stuff! China makes and exports an amazing range of products — in 2013 they shipped out US$2.2 trillion-worth. China is now the biggest trading nation and second-largest economy on the planet. It's also a massive shopping nation, expected to make up over a fifth of global consumer spending by 2020.

Workers look at a pattern in a textile factory.

High-Tech Wizards

Chinese workers are increasingly skilled, and gadgets make good money — electronic products such as computers, tablets and phones are now China's biggest exports. Over 90 per cent of all PCs and 70 per cent of mobiles are made in this country!

China makes more than a billion mobile phones a year!

Whopper Workforce

China has over 100 million manufacturing workers — about seven times more than the USA. Generally they work for much lower pay than those in the West, though wages have begun to rise.

Fashions & Feet

China's clothing exports bring in billions of dollars annually. The biggest sellers are knitted garments. China makes more than 8 billion pairs of socks and 12 billion pairs of shoes in a year – enough for everyone in the world to have a set, and more!

Many global brands make shoes in China.

Toys for All

Chinese factories produce three-quarters of the world's toys. Check out the labels on stuff you've got at home – you'll soon see what we're talking about!

NO WAY!

China now has more billionaires (152 in 2014) than any other country except the USA (492).

Big Buyers

The Chinese are brand-conscious, fashion-savvy and some of the biggest buyers of luxury goods, from designer bags to services such as health spas. Increasing numbers of people can afford to shop, making the country a high consumer. The world's two largest shopping malls are in China. Chinese tourists are also some of the biggest spenders abroad.

China's new shopping malls are full of luxury goods.

Be a Sport

The Chinese are disciplined and determined – and this shows when it comes to sport. The country has produced a string of world-class athletes and topped the bill with 51 gold medals at the Beijing Olympic Games. The government leads fitness-drives and people are embracing a wide range of sports, from golf to basketball and football. Meanwhile, traditional sports and games live on.

NO WAY!

The 1,000-year old sport of cricket fighting is still a big thing today. Pairs of the insects do battle until one runs away or stops chirping – the good news is, they rarely get harmed!

Tough Training

Sport isn't a traditional subject in Chinese schools, but it is becoming increasingly popular. Schemes are underway to improve football, volleyball and other PE lessons. In 2014, China's Ministry of Education joined with America's NBA to promote basketball skills. Meanwhile, children as young as four may be sent to elite (and controversial) sports academies, for intensive, high-level training.

You might see people practising gymnastics in playgrounds or on the street.

Table Tennis

Table tennis is really popular in China, and few people in the world can beat their professional players. After a clean sweep of medals in the 2008 Olympics (China won gold, silver and bronze in both men's and women's!), the rules were changed so that countries can enter only two players in the singles event. Why are the Chinese so good? They train HARD.

China's Wang Hao (right) and Zhang Jike on their way to victory in the men's table tennis final against South Korea at the 2012 Olympics.

Traditional Sports

China's martial arts, or kung fu, are world-famous – largely thanks to the 1970s movie star Bruce Lee! Styles including Shaolin, Tai Chi and Qigong have keen followers across the globe. The Chinese often perform kung fu in vast, perfectly synchronized groups. Racing wooden boats, carved and painted with dragon heads, is another ancient sport that attracts gigantic crowds.

Dragon boat racing is a 2,000- year-old pastime in China!

Land of the Panda

We all know that China is famous for its pandas - until quite recently, it was a tradition to give one away whenever a foreign leader came to visit! But giant pandas are endangered in the wild, found only in a few Chinese mountain regions. You can spot some other interesting and rare species here too.

The giant panda is a fussy eater, spending about 12 hours a day munching almost only bamboo! Pandas have a special bamboo-tearing thumb and a mucus-lined gut to protect against splinters. They also poo a lot.

The cat-sized red panda has a big bushy tail that wraps around like a blanket for sleeping. Like its giant cousin, it lives mainly in mountain regions – but it differs by making its home in trees. Deforestation is a danger for this shy animal.

For the Chinese symbol of happiness, good luck, long life and nobility, look for the red-crowned crane. You can often spot this elegant bird in Chinese art and embroidery.

It's not hard to see how the golden snub-nosed monkey got its name. This sociable creature likes to live in groups of hundreds, high in forest branches. Its luxurious fur keeps out the cold, but is also highly prized by hunters.

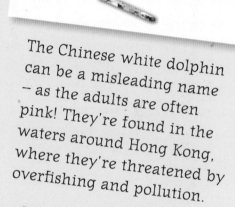

The Chinese white dolphin can be a misleading name – as the adults are often pink! They're found in the waters around Hong Kong, where they're threatened by overfishing and pollution.

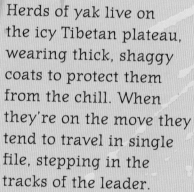

Herds of yak live on the icy Tibetan plateau, wearing thick, shaggy coats to protect them from the chill. When they're on the move they tend to travel in single file, stepping in the tracks of the leader.

Native to China, the ginkgo biloba is one of the oldest living tree species. Its leaf extract is used in traditional medicine, to promote brain health and improve memory among other things.

Believe It!

From religion to superstitions, the Chinese are strong believers. They see themselves as descendants of the dragon, so this creature is a symbol of good luck. Qi is the life force – a flow of energy said to affect all living things. And feng shui, linked to the wind and water, means arranging buildings, doors and furniture in just the right way to make you happy, healthy and even rich!

The Leshan Giant Buddha stands 71m tall – don't tread on his toes!

Religious Mix

With its communist rule, China is officially an atheist country. But religion has long played a part in Chinese culture. Buddhists are the biggest group, and proud guardians of the tallest stone Buddha in the world. Others are followers of Islam, folk religions or Taoisim – a philosophical, peace-loving faith. There are also fast-growing numbers of Christians. More people go to church on Sundays in China than across the whole of Europe!

Lucky You

If the money in your red envelope has an 8 in the total, that's extra lucky!

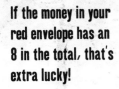

You CAN make luck, according to the Chinese! Wear red – it's the luckiest colour. Give a friend money in a red envelope – it'll bring good fortune. Get a lucky 8 in your phone number, but steer clear of dodgy digits: 4 is the worst (the word for it sounds like 'death'). You'll find floors 4, 14 and so on missing from some tall buildings, and 4 is unlikely to appear on a door or car number plate.

Animal Calendar

Rat, tiger, monkey, snake... everyone in China is linked to one of 12 animals, depending on which year they were born. The animals have different character types, and also tell you which other signs you might get on well with. China's calendar starts in January or February with a huge Spring (or New Year) Festival. It's a national holiday and a time for lavish costumes, parties and parades.

A good festival dragon has a lot of people underneath it!

NO WAY!

It's no accident that the opening ceremony of the Beijing Olympic Games began at 8 seconds and 8 minutes past 8 on 8-8-2008!

Let's Eat Together

Bigger is better in China — so if you dine with a native family, expect to be offered more than you can eat. Meals revolve around a shared spread of dishes, with tea and rice or noodles alongside. There are plenty of dips and sauces, and soup is usually served after the main course. Don't be surprised to find eyeballs, pig brains or duck's tongue on a plate — nothing is wasted here!

NO WAY!

China goes through about 80 billion pairs of disposable chopsticks a year – enough to cover Tiananmen Square over 360 times!

Taste Changes

Chinese cooking varies wherever you go. In the south, try rice porridge (congee) for breakfast with tofu, salted eggs or fish. Beijing is famous for duck pancakes and bird's nest soup, made with swallow spit. In Sichuan province, food is spicy, while Canton is known for its dim sum (bite-sized eats). Pork is popular everywhere – the Chinese eat 50 million tonnes of it a year.

Dim sum dumplings can be steamed or fried.

Rice is eaten throughout the day in China, including at breakfast time.

Everyone has their own rice bowl and spoon, plus a set of chopsticks. The most respected person starts first. It's normal to hold the bowl close to your mouth and use chopsticks to scoop food in. You shouldn't spear food with chopsticks, twiddle, point or tap them or stand them upright in your bowl. Slurping is a sign of enjoying your meal, and if you find a bone it's fine to spit it out.

Scary Snacks

Western fast food is popular in cities, along with some scarier street snacks...

deep-fried lizards, crickets, scorpions and centipedes – all served on a stick

roasted silkworm pupae

crunchy starfish or seahorse

stinky tofu – fermented for a tangy flavour

shredded donkey burger

In 2010, the first vending machine to sell live crabs was set up in a subway station near Nanjing.

Crickets

Scorpions and seahorses

Starfish

More Information

Websites

http://www.roughguides.com/destinations/asia/china

http://www.lonelyplanet.com/china
All you need to prepare for a trip to China.

http://www.bbc.co.uk/news/world-asia-pacific-13017877
An overview of China with facts and a timeline.

https://www.cia.gov/library/publications/the-world-factbook/geos/ch.html
The CIA World Factbook China page, with up-to-date info and statistics.

http://travel.nationalgeographic.com/travel/countries/china-guide
A profile of China, with photographs.

http://www.timeforkids.com/destination/china
A China guide with language tips and an interactive map.

Apps

Google Earth by Google, inc Explore China (and the rest of the world) from the sky – for free!

China Travel Guide by Triposo A bundle of background info, city guides, maps and phrasebooks.

Learn Chinese Free by Bravolol Unlimited Pick up the lingo with a colourful Mandarin-speaking parrot!

Building the Great Wall of China by Nordcurrent Take charge of building the Great Wall in this exciting, fast-paced game!

Clips

http://video.nationalgeographic.com/video/exploreorg/china-great-wall-eorg
All about the Great Wall and its construction.

http://video.nationalgeographic.com/video/exploreorg/china-terra-cotta-warriors-eorg
Meet Emperor Qin's army of Terracotta Warriors.

https://www.youtube.com/watch?v=WHxgls-R22Q
Watch Chinese children practise kung fu!

https://www.youtube.com/watch?v=w20UnLqTG8s
A snippet of Chinese opera.

https://www.youtube.com/watch?v=b53nK7S3ibE
A Chinese variety performance.

https://www.youtube.com/watch?v=GOL2eZtp2VO
Chinese contortionists in action.

Movies

Crouching Tiger, Hidden Dragon (12) This world-famous tale of warriors in 19th-century China is a dazzling display of martial arts skills.

The Karate Kid (PG) A bullied boy in China becomes an expert in kung fu.

Kung Fu Panda (PG) A comedy cartoon panda becomes a kung fu warrior.

Beijing Bicycle (PG) Lives in rural and urban China collide in this story about two boys and a bike.

Books

China (Countries Around the World) - Patrick Catel
(Raintree, 2013)

China (Countries in our World) - Oliver James
(Franklin Watts, 2013)

Not for Parents China: Everything You Ever Wanted to Know
(Lonely Planet Not for Parents, 2013)

Great Civilisations: Shang Dynasty China - Tracey Kelly
(Franklin Watts, 2014)

Hands on History! Ancient China - Philip Steele
(Armadillo Books, 2013)

Chinese Myths and Legends - Anita Ganeri
(Raintree, 2013)

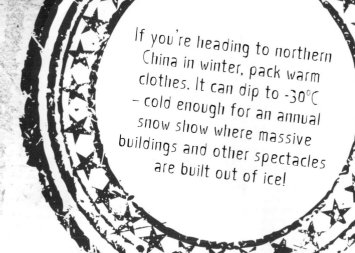

If you're heading to northern China in winter, pack warm clothes. It can dip to -30°C – cold enough for an annual snow show where massive buildings and other spectacles are built out of ice!

Glossary

atheist Someone who lacks belief in God or gods.

bamboo A tall, woody plant from the grass family.

civilization An organized society with systems of government, culture, industry and so on.

communist Following a system where all property and industry is owned by the community, rather than by individuals.

consumer Someone who buys goods and services for personal use.

deforestation Clearing trees to create space for activities such as farming or building, or to use the logs.

export To send goods abroad for sale.

mahjong A traditional Chinese game, usually played by four people, using 144 small tiles based on Chinese characters.

martial arts Sports that originated in China and some other Asian countries as a form of self defence.

metropolis A large, important city.

pilgrims People who travel to a sacred place for religious reasons.

smog A fog or haze created by air pollution.

superstition A belief in things that can't be logically explained, such as magic or the supernatural.

Index